I0116208

Kingdom
of
Heaven

Professor Hilton Hotema

ISBN: 978-1-63923-121-8

Printed: January 2022

Cover Art By: Paul Amid

Published and Distributed By:
Lushena Books
607 Country Club Drive, Unit E
Bensenville, IL 60106
www.lushenabks.com

ISBN: 978-1-63923-121-8

Kingdom of Heaven

Professor Hilton Hotema

Table of Contents

Chapter No.1
What Is A Kingdom

According to the church, the Kingdom of Heaven, Kingdom of God, and Spiritual World are synonymous. We shall show that there is a vast difference in all three.

Wm. McCarthy says that the Bible contains approximately thirty pages devoted exclusively to explanation of the Kingdom of God, and not one church presents a description of that Kingdom which coincides with the scriptures. A kingdom, according to the dictionary, is "The dominion of a monarch." It is usually the empire of a tyrant; the realm of a despot.

When the church fathers prepared their Bible, they invented an anthropomorphic God to head their religious system, and this God had to have a kingdom. Being the greatest of all tyrants, it was fitting and proper that he have the greatest of all kingdoms.

So the church made him the despotic ruler of the whole earth, and then, no doubt for the sake of safety, placed his Capitol, his Throne, his Seat of Power, in the Kingdom of Heaven, — wherever that is.

According to the church, this God "is a massive being, sitting in a marble chamber, studded with gold, and lighted with glistening crystals," wrote Joseph Lewis (Tyranny of God, 1921, p. 13). He added: "The most frightful and torturous instruments ever conceived by man, are those that were made (by the church) to force people to 'believe in God.' The history of religious persecution and torture is the horror of the world" (p. 120).

According to the church Bible, this God has all the traits and attributes of man. He insisted on and delighted in sacrifices and burnt-offerings; he was angry, jealous, revengeful, as well as wavering and irresolute; he allowed Moses to reason him out of his fixed resolution utterly to destroy his people; and he commanded the performance of the most shocking and hideous acts of cruelty and barbarity. That is a brief biblical picture of the church God; and if we do not believe in him, there is no end to the most terrible consequences that will befall us.

In the New Testament there appears an entirely different story of the Kingdom of God. The author of the John gospel made his Jesus say, "Except a man be born again, he cannot see the Kingdom of God — Except a man be born of water and of the Spirit, he cannot enter into the Kingdom of God" (Jn. 3:3, 5).

If the Kingdom of God does not include everything, who is the ruler of that part not included? And if we do not live in the Kingdom of God, where are we? That Kingdom mentioned in the John gospel must have been located far off in some secret corner of the Universe, and as unknown to the Jesus of the Matthew and Mark gospels, in which he was made to say: "Whereunto shall I liken the Kingdom of God, or with what comparison shall we compare it? It is like a grain of mustard seed, which, when sown in the earth, is less that all the seeds that be in the earth, but when sown, it groweth up, and becometh greater than all herbs, and shooteth out great branches; so that the fowls of the air may lodge under the shadow of it" (Mat. 13:31; Mk. 4:31).

The author of Luke made his Jesus give a more definite description: "The Kingdom of God cometh not with observation; neither shall they say, Lo here! or lo there! for, behold the Kingdom of God is within you" (Lu. 17:21). A vast difference between that Kingdom and the Kingdom of the Church.

Then Paul describes the Kingdom of God. He said, "For the kingdom of God is not meat and drink, but righteousness, and peace, and joy" (Rom. 14:17). According to that description, the Kingdom is not a place in space, but a state of Mind.

It is not difficult to reconcile the statement of Paul with those of the three synoptic gospels; but the statements in the John, no doubt interpolated by some ignorant monk, harmonize only with absurdity and stupidity.

Grand Cosmic Kingdom

In the ancient arcane science, Spirit was the basis of all things. The basis of spirit was polarized and intelligized atoms, and "dead" matter did not exist. Even the stone vibrates.

The various kingdoms of the cosmos are manifestations of the Grand Cosmic Kingdom. They descend from the Spiritual to the Mineral, as vibration decreases and density increases, as follows to-wit: 1. Spiritual 2. Mental 3. Astral 4. Angelic 5. Animalistic 6. Vegetal 7. Angelic.

Man dwells in the Animalistic Kingdom while ruled by his animal nature; and he rises to the Angelic Kingdom when convinced that he is a god. Such neither marry, nor are given in marriage; but are (free of animal passions) as the angels (Mk. 12:25). This is what Paul meant when he said: "They that have wives be as though they had none" (1 Cor. 7:29).

Man is the greatest organized intelligence on earth, the greatest of all creatures, and he may rise to the highest plane of being, or sink lower than the beast.

True Being is fixed and eternal. Existence is an emanation into the visible world of becoming, of constant change and transformation, and in this state man is swayed, influenced, ruled by emotions, according to conditions, regardless of right or wrong. The trend is up or down, and will correspond in results in exact proportions to the work of the "Guard at the Gate."

Through this Gate must pass all Thoughts to and from the Spiritual Kingdom, which Thoughts always precede action, and always produce their Kind. We think before we act; and as a Man thinketh, so is he (Pr. 23:7). Through this Gate all things are made possible; and through this Gate man may make himself a God or a Beast.

Freedom

The Animal Kingdom is ruled by Instinct, and is confined to certain bounds, which animals cannot exceed nor go beyond. Man is a free agent, bound by no conditions but of his own work. His high destiny demands freedom from all restraint.

Man, kept in darkness and ignorance, knows little of his high estate. He is made subject to all manner of enslaving influences, and is more or less at the mercy of those who dominate leadership for good or evil. This man in darkness gives away his high estate and accepts the dictates of others.

Man's position in the Grand Scale of the Cosmic Pattern typifies Freedom. But that Freedom is conditional, not absolute. It must be so. Otherwise, Life would be a fixed stage — predestination — and man would have no choice. Freedom is the one and only basis fitting into the Cosmic Plan of Life for Man.

In Freedom is man's birthright and divine estate. It rests with him alone as to whether he will sell it for a "mess of pottage," give it away, or keep it, and cultivate it, and make it produce for him that which it alone can bring — the greatest of all attainments.

The fact that millions are in Mental Bondage, in one form or another, is proof that Real Freedom is little known. The reason of this Mental Bondage is darkness, ignorance, trickery, fraud, deception, etc. The multitude lives in the fifth sense, the power of sight, and is easily misled. Some have reached the higher state of this sense, from which flow flashes of knowledge, so much in use for gain, oppression, selfishness, evil.

"Knowledge wrongly applied is dangerous."

The Bible warns man of the dangers of living by sight. He is urged to look not at things which are seen, but at things which are not seen, "For things seen are temporal; but things not seen with the eyes, but in the Mind, are eternal" (2 Cor. 4:18).

A few persons are in the sixth sense. They have advanced

above the multitude, and realize the folly and error of the race as a whole. A very small number have risen to the seventh sense. For the sake of safety, they conceal that fact. They have no desire to join the ranks of those mighty men who have been persecuted, assassinated, burned. Those in the sixth sense know dimly what the seventh is like, and look forward to the time when they will have attained that high level. They also know that its attainment by the masses is a dream never to be realized.

Man's freedom of choice, mixed with certain knowledge, is binding millions to illusionary ideals called wealth and power. These illusions, reacting on lower levels, produce abnormal desires and vicious tendencies, so prevalent in civilization.

Conscience

"They heard the voice of God walking in the garden" (Gen. 3:8). A guilty Conscience needs no accuser. The "Still Small Voice" is not one of "sound." There is no need of noise.

The "Voice Within" dictates our every move. Some say its seat is in the emotional center of the Solar Plexus, and term it Conscience. Conscience is the receiving instrument of the body. Conscience, under certain conditions, is the dictator of our every mood, conduct, and act. In this respect we act from the "Voice of Conscience," the "Still Small Voice."

There is another factor — the Ego, or Guard at the Gate. It is closely associated with Conscience, but is not Conscience itself. While all powerful, yet it is passive, even unto being subordinated by Conscience. Aside from the Guard at the Gate, Conscience becomes the dictator throughout Life.

But Conscience changes. As we grow older and fall into the habits of the race, conscience becomes blunt and hardened. That which would make the Conscience of a properly raised youth recoil in horror, later becomes common place, and even accepted.

Chapter No.2
Mind

Man is a thinker. Until recently, the world's philosophers had classed all his mental activities in one group. Whatever man thought, they said he thought with his "Mind." But in the 19th century, certain advanced psychologists began to make a distinction between those thought processes of which man was conscious, and those of which he was no conscious.

They observed, for example, that in picking up a stone and throwing it at a mark he used conscious, choosing mental activity; but that in walking, he did not consciously move one foot after the other, he simply walked, without consciously thinking of it.

He could be using his conscious thought processes in reading, while unconsciously moving his legs in walking. During the daytime, he would be thinking consciously of his various activities, but when he fell asleep he was not thinking consciously.

Yet, in his dreams he was having experiences, perhaps traveling to a far place, or being chased by an angry bull. The experience was a thought process, but it was not consciously selected and performed. This led close observers to make a distinction between what they termed "conscious" mind and "subconscious" mind, or the conscious and subconscious phases of one mind. These terms are now being replaced by the words "objective for conscious, and "subjective" for subconscious.

Objective Mind

Objective Mind is that phase which reasons, chooses, observes, judges, estimates, and decides. Its chief characteristic is the "power of choice."

Subjective Mind

Subjective mind never reasons. It obeys the choice of the objective mind. It is the servant of objective mind. Yet its power and scope are far greater; for it is estimated that 90% of our mental activities are subjective. It is as though a giant slave were following the directions of a child of a slaveholder. All his vast strength would be entirely at the child's service, to lift and move more heavy objects that the child's strength could not budge.

Subjective mind is highly intelligent, but it does not reason. Its intelligence is perfect. It knows how to do all things. It has all knowledge. It knows how to create anything that ever was created. It knows how to build a body, for it built every body that was ever built. Subjective mind knows how to make supply flow in the right direction. It knows how to keep the heart beating, the blood circulating, the cells working. It keeps the nerves in condition to transmit lightning messages from one part of the body to another.

Subjective mind is the worker that has created every objective thing in the universe.

Microcosm and Macrocosm

The same creative process and the same creative substance by which a world is constructed are used in building man. By coming to a clear understanding of that fact, man can change his little world. We think of a trinity in man, as Spirit, Mind and Body, and see these as a Cosmic Trinity. We may think of creation as the making of something out of nothing, which is erroneous. It is the process of transforming Invisible Substance into Visible forms, under the Law of Polarity.

Cosmic Mind

Some hold that there is only One Mind. That same Mind which formed the granite mountain formed the grass of the field and the body of Man. This One Mind is regarded as a great, invisible sea, pervading and penetrating the entire universe.

Leading out of this fact is the second important truth, which is that which man calls 'his' subjective mind is merely that portion of this Great Mind which he is using at any particular time.

Therefore, man has at his instantaneous disposal the greatest power in the universe. It is entirely subject to his will, and will work obediently for him in a constructive way when he understands how to direct its course in the proper channel. And it will work just as obediently for him in a destructive way when he fails to guide it properly.

Why People Fail

If this is all true, and man has at his command such a tremendous flow of power, waiting to be directed toward the solution of his problems of life, the logical question which arises is, "Then why does anyone ever fail?"

Here is a statement of fact as to the availability of unlimited assistance, yet on every side we see people struggling weakly in the grasp of circumstances, praying to an imaginary God to lighten their loads, running hither and thither seeking some way of escape, and giving way to the blankness of despair.

What a bleak picture! Man, the Lord of the whole Earth, with dominion over every living thing, scourged by his fears and cringing in a dark corner, while the bugs, birds and beasts go merrily on, living in harmony with the Law of Life.

Mind Control

The reason why people fail is clear and obvious to one who makes a rational investigation of the matter. Mind makes Man. Control the Mind and you control the Man. Enlighten the Mind and you enlighten the Man. Blank the Mind and you blank the Man. Fifty per cent of the masses are almost blank. Twenty-five per cent are partially blank. Psychological tests conducted on the soldiers in World War I showed that the mental development of the average man is no higher than that of a 13-year old child.

Science has shown that the best of us use less than ten per

cent of our brain capacity. The inevitable is that we are all at least 90% ignorant. It is hard to believe that we know so little about ourselves and our world in which we live. Conscious Mind is limited and deluded by the Five Senses. It is controlled by theology, by the church, by education and training, and by the orthodox social pattern. Get out of step with these and you become an outcast on earth. That is why people fail.

Freedom and Slavery

As the Roman Catholic Church completely controls the Mind of its members, that completely and certainly are they enslaved. The church tells them what they may read and what they may think. Protestants have little more freedom, as their Mind is not so completely controlled by the church.

The freest are the Free-thinkers; yet they are less free than they think. For the Mind of most of them is bound by the stupid theories of modern science regarding Man, Life, and God, and by the preposterous theories of medical art that the world is filled with "diseases" which are trying to destroy the race.

The condition called civilization is controlled, artificial mode of living that weakens and degenerates the human organism. The first powers lost are the higher and more delicate powers of the brain. Under the law of compensation, man cannot live the controlled life of artificialism without sacrificing the virtues of naturalism; and it is that naturalism which enables the bugs, birds and beasts to live in harmony with the law of their being.

The chief factor that leads to human failure is the rule of authority. Under that rule man lives a controlled, artificial life that inhibits brain development. He is not permitted to think. His thinking is done for him by the so-called authorities. These authorities rule all human conduct in civilization. Man is told what he can do and what he cannot do.

In religious matters; the authority is the church. In all other cases, the authority abides in the various law-making bodies, from the smallest city council up to the national congress. By these authorities civilized man is ruled as with a rod of iron. That has been his status for so many ages, that 90% of his brain cells are dormant, and so declared by modem science.

One's teaching may be in harmony with the Cosmic Plan of Life, the Law of Perfection, and the Science of Natural Economy. But that teaching docs not harmonize with civilization's artificial world, nor support its social pattern, nor its organized instructions, therefore it cannot be accepted and supported by an institution or any form of government. It must be suppressed "for the good of the people."

Tell us how long man's created wants and unnatural desires will mean money for Commercialism, and we will tell you how long man will remain in his present condition of mental degeneracy and economic slavery.

Chapter No.3
Mental Kingdom

Sir James Jeans wrote: "All the choir of heaven and all the furniture of earth have no existence outside of Mind" *(Mysterious Universe.)* Dr. Gustav Stromberg said: "The only thing I can imagine that is behind Matter, or that is more fundamental than Matter is Mind. Mind is probably the button of everything" *(Soul of the Universe.)* Modern science takes the opposite view. It attributes greater reality to Matter than to Mind; and all branches of science neglect to study the various aspects of Consciousness.

Mind, the Kingdom within, is little know and never described by the clergy. It is entirely neglected by theologists, physiologist, economists, and almost unnoticed by physicians.

And yet this neglected and little known Mental Kingdom Within expands as brain develops and consciousness increases until, like that grain of mustard see, it grows and becomes the greatest, highest, the most colossal power in the Universe.

One of the most mysterious phenomena in life of the human organism is the life-history of brain-cells. They do not multiply as the cells of other tissues do. According to one theory, brain-cells all appear at a very early age. According to another, they grow in number until the organism has reached the age of puberty. But how they grow, and out of what they grow, remains unknown.

We have said that Objective Mind is conscious mind, and

is limited by man's state of consciousness which, as a rule, depends on his five faulty sense powers, concerning which Emerson said: "The influence of the senses has, in most men, overpowered the Mind to that degree, that the walls of Time and Space have come to look real, solid, and unsurmountable." (p. 167)

And so it is. With his five faulty senses, man builds his world, making it lie within his power to build his world as largely or as little as he likes. He may expand his World by improving his senses and expanding his consciousness; but that course is dangerous for the church and for all established institutions; and so mind improvement and consciousness expansion are opposed.

Mind Power is potentially omnipotent, omnipresent, and omniscient. It rises to the sky, to infinity, to eternity, even in the average man. Nothing can bar its way. It penetrates steel as well as space; it crosses the Time-Space barrier, and Time is not more. (Rev. 10:6) The old man looks back into the past, and sees himself as a boy in the old swimming hole. The engineer gazes into the future, and sees the skyscraper he plans to build, filled with goods and people. Thus the future and the past merge and become the eternal Present. Sight and sound are limited by brain power, not by distance. The eagle can see farther, and the dog can hear farther and smell better, than most men, — due to man's defective brain development and its deterioration.

Mind can measure distances and count light years. It calculates astronomical cycles, sizes and densities. It invents telescopes to peer into space, discovers millions of suns, planets, and universes, measures cosmic rays and light waves, traps electricity, and finds ways and means to circle the earth on wings of metal. By the aid of telephone and radio man can talk around the world; and by the aid of television he can see things miles away. Full consciousness is great clearness and vividness of the five senses. Super-consciousness is that rare state which rises from a conjunction of Objective and the Subjective Mind, and which results from an actuation of the mysterious sixth and seventh sense powers, to be noticed later.

The Ancient Masters believed that beyond the reach of man's five faulty senses there existed a vast ocean almost entirely unexplored, and yet filled with forces, actions, objects, and meaning, all relating to atomic forms, mind substance, thought waves, and spiritual activity. Anaximenes (380 - 320 B.C.) said: "The Essence of the Universe is in the Infinite Air in eternal movement which contains ALL in itself. Everything is formed (not created) by the integration and disintegration of the Essence of the Air under the Law of Expansion and Contraction."

This invisible Essence of the Universe, composed of the most important and mysterious forces and elements dealing with man, are as yet little known to modern science, and the existence of some is even denied. The Ancient Masters postulated that all these cosmic phenomena and elements are possessed by man, that he is the Microcosm of the Macrocosm, and so indicated when they said, "That which is above is like that which is below."

With all of these cosmic phenomena man is connected by Mind, as expressed by Bergson, a French philosopher, who regarded Mind as potentially omniscient, aware of everything, everywhere. He said, "The brain is the reducing valve that makes Universal Mind available to man." Mind presents two phases, the Objective (Conscious), and the Subjective (Unconscious or Subconscious.) To a limited extent, the Subjective obeys the orders of the Objective and acts as its servant.

But 90% of man's mental functions are subjective. Also, the Subjective carries on its work at all times without interruption, whether man is awake or asleep. We speak of God Mind, Divine Mind, Cosmic Mind, One Mind, etc., but those who so designate it, never describe it nor locate it.

We may learn something if we examine the subject from the standpoint of reason and common sense. Let us forget some imaginary God for the moment and examine the atom. One writer has said that "Absolute Intelligence thrills through every Atom of the world. What, is the source or origin of that Intelligence? Thomas Edison, the great inventor, tells us. He is reported by an interviewer as having said in Harper's Magazine for February 1890 as follow:

"To me, it seems that every atom is possessed by a certain amount of primitive intelligence. Look at the thousands of ways in which atoms of hydrogen combine with those of other elements, forming the most diverse substances. Do you mean to say that the atoms do this without intelligence? Atoms in harmonious and definite relation assume beautiful and interesting shapes and colors, or emit a pleasant perfume, as if expressing their satisfaction. Collected in certain forms, the atoms constitute animals of the lower order. Finally, they combine to form man, who represents the total intelligence of

all the atoms (in his body.)"

Who will draw the line between Mind and Intelligence? Where can it be drawn? In a longer interview, quoted in the Scientific American in 1920, Edison expressed a number of opinions, from which are excerpted the following: 1. Life, like matter, is indestructible. 2. Our bodies are composed of myriads of infinitesimal entities, each in itself a unit of life; just as the atom is composed of myriads of electrons. 3. The human being acts as an assemblage rather than as a unit. The body and mind express the vote or voice of the life entities. 4. The life entities build according to a plan. If a part of the living organism be mutilated, they rebuild exactly as before. 5. The life entities live forever; so to that extent at least the eternal life for which many of us hope, is a reality. What are these "life entities?" *The atoms*.

Sir Wm. Crookes, one of the greatest scientists, gave an interesting lecture in 1895 before a body of chemists in Great Britain, in which he dealt with the ability of the atom to choose its own path, to *reject* and to *select*, and showed that natural selection can be traced in all living forms, from the atom up through all forms of being. In another scientific article, the atom was further said to have the power of volition and sensation, thus completing the four points of the Cross of Life.

So, it appears that the atom is a living entity, a little vibrant world, possessing the qualities of intelligence and the ability to select and reject, to attract and repulse, sensation, movement.

Many thousands of years ago, the Ancient Masters said,

"Every form on earth, and every speck in space, strives in its efforts toward self-formation, and to follow the model placed for it in the Divine Man. The involution and the evolution of the atom . . . . have all one and the same object: — man."

These Masters declared, *"Know Thyself, for in Thyself is to be found all that there is to be known."*

Chapter No.4
Consciousness

We have mentioned two phases of Consciousness, one phase of which is subject to the Will, while the other is not. Consciousness is another mystery, the greatest and most profound of all mysteries. The word Consciousness is unique. It is a coined English word; its equivalent appears not in other languages, and was not used by the Ancient Masters.

The word Consciousness is formed by the union of two Latin words: con-with, and scio-to know; and literally means *"That with which we know"* Some authors list three types of consciousness, as (1) Absolute consciousness, (2) Universal consciousness, and (3) Individual consciousness. The first is defined as, "That consciousness in which everything is, the possible as well as the actual." This may be termed the basic consciousness of the atom.

Universal consciousness may be defined as thinking time and space, consciousness with the idea of location and succession involved within it, or, in reality, atomic group consciousness, the group of atoms itself forming either a greater or lesser unit.

Individual consciousness may be defined as just as much of universal consciousness as a separate unit can contact and conceive of for itself. Individual consciousness to the atom in man's body would be its own vibratory life, its own internal activity, and all that specifically concerns itself.

Universal consciousness to the cell might be considered as the consciousness of the entire body, viewing it as the unit which incorporates the atom. Absolute consciousness to the atom might be considered as the consciousness of the thinking man who is energizing the body. To the atom that would be something so remote to its own internal life as to be practically inconceivable and unknown, yet it sweeps into the line of its will the form and the atom in the form, and all that concerns them.

Ancient esoteric philosophy held that consciousness must be predicated not only of the animal and of man, but must be recognized as extending through the vegetable on into the mineral kingdom, and that self-consciousness must be regarded as the consummation of the evolutionary growths of consciousness in the three lower kingdoms. And here, in the tiny atom, that reservoir of tremendous power, we find the seat and center of the great mystery and the end of the long trail.

The atom is the life unit, the intelligence unit, the building unit, and the building material. The atom is the God Mind, the Divine Mind, the Universal Mind, the Word-Soul, and the Over-Soul of Emerson, "within which every man's particular being is contained and made one with all other;" the church God who is all and is in all, and who is made to say in the Bible, "Let us make man in our image." (Gen. 1.26)

And here at last we have found the Kingdom of God described in the Bible, — that grain of mustard seed, which, when sown in the earth, is less than all the seeds that be in the earth; but when sown, it groweth up, and becometh greater (and mightier) than all herbs, and shooteth out great branches; so that the fowls of the air may lodge under the shadow of it.

(Mat. 13:31; Mk. 4:31)

Super Consciousness

It has been recognized that we must not regard the common state of consciousness in man as the only possible one.

It has been well-established that there are higher states of consciousness, which are rare and have been studied very little, and in which we learn and understand things that we cannot learn and understand in ordinary state of consciousness.

This serves to establish the fact that the common state of consciousness is only a particular instance of consciousness, and that our ordinary conception of the world is only a particular instance of conception of the world.

The study of these rare and exceptional states of consciousness of man have established a certain unity, a certain connectedness and consecutiveness, and an entirely illogical "logicalness," in the content of the so-called "mystical" state of consciousness. An examination of what is known as mysticism and mystical states of consciousness is of exceptional interest in connection with the idea of "hidden" knowledge.

In relation to the idea of "hidden" knowledge, mysticism can be regarded as a breaking through into man's consciousness of this "hidden" knowledge. It appears to be a union of the objective consciousness with the subjective consciousness, producing what may properly be termed a state of Super-Consciousness.

We have said that the Subjective Mind knows how to do all things and has all knowledge. In the ritual of the Ancient Mysteries the neophyte was taught how to draw the Subjective Mind into the Objective Mind, and allow the Omniscient Power of the Subjective to flow into the Objective.

That is the secret of the Book with Seven Seals mentioned in the Bible; which no man in heaven, nor in earth, neither under the earth, was able to open, neither to look thereon. (Rev. 5:1-3) *The Magic Wand* was the symbol of this secret, as shown in our work under that title. Mysticism could not exist without "hidden" knowledge, and the idea of "hidden" knowledge could not be known without mysticism.

"Hidden" knowledge is an idea that does not fit into any other. The ability to contact "hidden" knowledge appears in certain people, in people whom we do not know, in what may be termed an inner circle of humanity.

All the exoteric history of humanity that we know, is the history of the outer circle. Within this circle there is another, of which those of the outer circle know nothing, and the existence of which they only dimly suspect. Yet the life of the outer circle and particularly in its evolution, is actually guided by the inner circle.

The inner or esoteric circle forms, as it were, a life within life, a mystery, a secret in the life of humanity, a divine state which science refuses to investigate, and a state which the masses have never reached and never will reach. Instances of this divine state appear in cases of hypnotism, and many of them have been recorded. Littlefield mentions some of these cases in his work *"The Beginning and Way of Life."* He wrote: "In 1896, the author, while a member of a class of psychic research, had two boys, a white boy and a negro, for subjects, both of whom had, while under hypnotic control, the powers of clairvoyance and clairaudience to a remarkable degree.

"The colored boy could be sent (?) to any place the operator desired, to examine anything or any condition, in or out of the city, and not once in many test cases was he found to be mistaken.

"The white boy, although he had not gone beyond the eighth grade in school, could, while under hypnotic control, translate into the best English, Greek or Latin sentences of the most complicated kind. While both these boys could do many other remarkable things, these are sufficient to indicate the scope of their (superconscious) powers. Only two explanations are possible as to the manner in which this work is accomplished.

"In the case of the negro boy, the soul had the power to leave its physical fellow sitting blind-folded in my office, while it was absent on the requested errand, or it possessed means of obtaining the desired information without leaving the body. I believe the latter to be the true explanation.

"In the case of the white boy, the soul had the power to come enrapport with the mind of Clark Braden, the then noted Bible scholar and lecturer of the Christian Church, who conducted the experiments; or it possessed the faculty, activated by hypnotism, of receiving knowledge otherwise than by objective education. Here I also believe the latter to be true. In either explanation, no such phenomena would be possible without a *corresponding brain organ* through which these things could address the consciousness, for in no other way could the boys translate their super-conscious experiences into ideas common to the human mind, and thus bring the knowledge of the soul (subjective mind) within the realm of material things." – p. 284

The press of August 2, 1956, date-lined Trenton, New Jersey, reported the case of a lost safe combination that was recovered thru hypnotism. Shirley Weiss, age 22, was hypnotized by Alex Batyi, professional hypnotist, and taken back several years in her life to the day when she saw the combination written on a paper slip. The combination had been forgotten and the safe could not be opened. By this process the combination was recovered and the safe opened. Then there is the notorious case of Bridey Murphy that created such intense interest. This occurred in 1952, when Mrs. Ruth Simmons was hypnotized by Morey Bernstein, businessman of Pueblo, Colorado, who took up the study of hypnosis and became so proficient that he was able to help persons stop smoking and drinking. He was even able to end certain psychosomatic maladies such as stuttering and chronic headaches.

After he had put Mrs. Simmons in deep hypnotic trance, in the presence of witnesses, a home tape recorder was turned on.

The experiment began with what is termed the "age regression process." It means taking Mrs. S. back to the age of 7, to 5, to 3, to 1. At each age she recalled events of her life at that time, her playmates, the dolls she had at each age, and who sat in front and back of her at school. The experiment was going so well, that Bernstein decided to try what only a few hypnotists had attempted   to take his subject back beyond her birth, back even to a previous existence. So he said to Mrs. S.: "1 want you to keep going back, back through space and time, and you will find there are other scenes in your memory .... Now you are going to tell me what you see ..." In the presence of her husband and friends, she told of the life and death of Bridey Murphy.

She told of being born in Cork, Ireland, in 1798; of marrying a barrister named Brian, of moving to Belfast, of remembering songs and books and dances of that era. And finally, she remembered dying at the age of 66, after suffering a broken hip in a fall. Four times the "Bridey Murphy" experiment was undertaken in Pueblo. Each time Mrs. S. told the same story. Neither she nor Bernestein had ever been in Ireland.

Then there began the search for Bridey Murphy, the name by which Mrs. S. said she was known at that time.

The search was undertaken by Irish law firm, various librarians and investigators in Ireland, unknown to Mrs. S. They reported that many of the points in Mrs. S.'s story were correct, such as the names of the stores, a rope factory, a tobacco company that was in existence at the time she said she had lived there.

When the hypnotic test was ended, Mrs. S. said that she did not know nor remember one thing that she had said. When asked about it, without hesitation she replied: "I didn't know a thing about it until Morey played the tapes (tape recorder) back."

The divine state of Super consciousness is dealt with in the Bible in symbol and allegory that cannot be understood by the exoteric. How to attain it was the great work of the Ancient Mysteries. The first step in the task of preparing for initiation was the practice of rigid self-denial. If any man desires to attain the Divine State, let him deny himself, and follow me. (Mat. 16:24)

Man is transformed by a renewing of the Mind (Rom. 12:2,) and he who seeks the higher life must deny himself the so-called pleasures of the physical life, and trade the path that leads up-hill all the way, as described in our works *"The Great Red Dragon"* and *"The Magic Wand."*

Chapter No.5
Spiritual Organs

"Each part of the body seems to know the present and future needs of the whole, and acts accordingly. The significance of Time and Space is not the same for our Cells as for our (physical) Mind. The body perceives the remote as well as the near, the future as well as the present." (Carrel, in *"Man The Unknown,"* p. 197). Ancient writings are filled with references to the Spiritual World. Modern science holds that such world is a myth — that all is material substance and mechanical energy.

Ancient science taught that man is a miniature Universe (Microcosm.) Hence, if there is a Spiritual Realm in the Universe (Macrocosm,) there must also be one in man. If that be true, man's body must contain organs through which the Spiritual Realm may manifest itself on the material plane. Not long ago modern science regarded the air as empty and void. Thousands of years before the Masters taught that "the Essence of the Universe is in the Infinite Air in eternal movement which contains ALL in itself."

All animals exhibited strange powers. Hornets and wasps have always known how to make paper. They were never taught and needed no experience. Whence comes this knowledge?

Birds have always built their nests as they do now, and each kind builds a certain type of nest. They were never taught, and needed no experience. Whence comes this knowledge?

Birds know which way to travel and when, to avoid winter's icy blast. They know that snow and ice will come at a certain time and they must fly in a definite direction to a certain region to escape the fate of being frozen to death. Whence comes this knowledge? Modem science has no rational answer for these questions. The best it can do is to suggest that the birds and beasts are guided by "instinct." It fails to explain what "instinct" is, and assumes that it must be a property of Matter.

Materialism is a Superstition

Modern physics has studied phenomena in matter around us. That brand of physics died with the discovery of the electron. Physicists are now busy trying to make the electron fit their materialism. They refuse to understand that the electron belongs to another world — the Spiritual World of the Masters.

Radio, Radar and Television are mechanized examples of the Spiritual Powers that operate as Vital Intelligence in the strange conduct of birds and beasts, which science calls Instinct. Why does man not have these powers? The Ancient Masters taught that there is a Spiritual Realm in man. "The kingdom of God is within you. (Lu. 17:21) That includes everything and all. The Spiritual Realm in man is located in the Spiritual Chambers of the skull, called the Golden Bowl by the Masters. (Ecel. 12:6)

These Chambers, the function of which is unknown to modern science, are Five in number. The Masters called them the Five Stars of the Microcosm, and they are symbolized in ancient scriptures by certain fives, as the Five Golden Emerods (1 S. 6:4); the Five Loaves (Mat. 14:17), etc.

The Sankhys doctrine states that the Five Physical Senses of conscious man are the exteriorized products of the five corresponding Spiritual Centers, which are as follows:

1. FRONTAL SINUS – A cavity in the frontal bone of the skull.
2. SPHENOIDAL SINUS – A cavity in the sphenoid bone of the skull.
3. MAXILLARY SINUS – Largest of the five, and resembles a pyramid in shape.
4. PALATINE SINUS – A cavity in the orbital process of the palatine bone and opening into either the sphenoidal or a posterior ethmoidal sinus.
5. ETHMOIDAL SINUS – This chamber consists of numerous small cavities occupying the labyrinth of ethmoid bone, and in these cavities are situated the small, mysterious glands known in Occult Science as the Intellectual Organs.

The sinuses communicate directly or indirectly with the nasal cavity; and it is highly significant to observe that they receive the Breath of Life directly and unmodified as it flows from the Universe to them through the nose, and before any of the other organs have a chance to select and absorb any substance from the Spiritual Essence of the Cosmos, charged with every known and unknown element.

The Sinuses are lined with the mucous membrane extending into them from the nose, and to them rapidly spreads all disorders that affect the nose. They receive, without protection, the full charge of all poisonous gases and acids in the air. The nose is the first organ that reacts to polluted air, and that reaction is called a "cold." The inflammation resulting from the effect of the polluted air extends from the nasal mucous lining to that of the Sinuses, causing such disorders as frontal headache (frontal sinus), pain in the check (maxillary sinus), pain between the eyes (ethmoidal sinuses), and deep seated pain at back of eyes (spenoidal sinus). These aches and pains, indicating serious damage being done to these Spiritual Chambers, are caused by poisonous air entering the nostrils. The air may be so slightly polluted that it fails to produce the reaction called the "simple cold." Thus begins the destruction of the vital Spiritual Centers of man while he is only an infant – and when the truth is known, that "cold" is a sign of serious damage being done, and not so "simple" as some think.

The mucus excretions of the lining of the maxillary sinus, in inflammatory conditions, fill up this sinus, as the orifice is at the uppermost part. Such of the mucus as cannot be blown out through the nose, remains in the sinus where it gradually hardens, destroying the spiritual function of that chamber — the largest of the group.

Recovery From Illness Only Partial

Full recovery from ailments is a myth. Each one is a step down the ladder of degeneration to the grave at the bottom. If the illness is slight, the downward step is short. If severe, the downward step is longer. Recovering from each illness is only partial, regardless of how slight the illness may be. But if degeneration has not gone too far, a change in one's mode of living that brings the body in harmony with God's Law of Life, will result in Regeneration.

The sinuses superficially appear to some as nothing more than air chambers in the skull. They are ignorant of their true function, and assume that their purpose is to lend resonance to the voice.

The voice organ is in the throat, not in the nose nor in the sinuses. Occult Science, termed by modern science as "that school of stupid superstition," teaches that in these Spiritual Chambers is located the seat of the Intellectual Divinity of man.

These air chambers and the small glands in them constitute the spiritual sense-centers that receive the Higher Intelligence, which is too subtle for contact by the five physical senses of conscious man, in his present degenerate state. But this was not so when man enjoyed full Physical Perfection.

Into these chambers there incessantly flows a peculiar gaseous substance, a subtle essence, known to the Ancient Masters as Mental Spirit. It can produce no normal reaction in the spiritual chambers of civilized man, as they are deficient, dormant, degenerated by the evil work of polluted air. The small glands, the Intellectual Organs, located in the skull near the point where the nose joins the forehead, are activated by the Mental Spirit that passes through the nostrils into the ordinate and collaborate with the sinuses. This is the chief Spiritual Intelligent Center of man.

In wild birds and beasts, and the wild natives that have

not been tainted and tinged by the "blessings" of civilization, these spiritual centers are functionally developed — and modern science attempts to explain the uncanny powers of these creatures by asserting that they are guided by "instinct;" but we are not told what "instinct" is. If a hunting dog be kept in the house and breathe the polluted air the same as the members of the family, in time the nerves in the nose and sinuses become dull, the dog loses its keen sense of smell and is unable to trail game. Like causes produce like effects.

Some wild tribes are found that still posses the peculiar powers of wild birds and beasts. The polluted air of civilization has not reached them yet, and their centers of Cosmic Intelligence are not dormant and rendered practically useless by the destructive action of polluted air, in which civilized man lives and labors from birth to death.

Uncanny Powers of Indians

According to innumerable observers and historians, as well as Indian tradition, when the Spaniards arrived to take over South America, they found that the Incan races had an uncanny and super-natural ability for conveying and receiving accurate information over long distances. If we are to credit the apparently unvarnished accounts, it was as remarkable in its way as wireless telegraphy or mental telepathy.

An Indian could, and often did, know exactly how many men on horses were approaching long before they could be seen or heard. He could tell where or in which direction a friend or foe was traveling, and he could perform many more equally mysterious feats. Dr. Juan Durand, who devoted many years to a study of Indian history, traditions and life, personally witnessed such feats. One night, while at an Indian hut at Raco, the Indian owner placed his ear to the floor and told Dr. Durand the exact number of men in a platoon of soldiers who were passing at a distance of more than three kilometers from the spot.

Another Indian at Panao, without rising from his couch, stated the number of men on foot and the number of mounted men traveling on a distant road, and even told the order in which they moved and the direction in which they were going.

In 1896, while between Cayumba and Monson, Durand's Indian carries deserted. Other Indians, without faltering or hesitating, gave the exact route the deserters had taken and followed them for eight days across deserts, mountains and rivers where there was no sign of a trail or spoor, often cutting across country, and found the deserters exactly where they had foretold.

According to historians and to Dr. Durand, the Peruvian tribes were able to receive such information of distant events by their ability to "read" the barking and howling of their dogs, and that this knowledge of the dogs' language thus enabled them to receive information and full details of matters of which they would otherwise know nothing. In all probability this was merely an explanation to satisfy the curiosity of the white man.

An amazing demonstration of the miraculous powers once active in the body, but apparently dormant in civilized man, occurred in Czechoslovakia and was recently reported in the Magazine Digest. It appears two young men discovered that after certain vigorous breathing exercises in good, fresh air, they could make themselves into human radio receiving sets.

With nothing but a loud speaker, on which they put their hands, they could at will tune in any station within several hundred miles and bring in the music clearly through the loud speaker. They were investigated by reporters and professors, but no explanation could be offered except the breathing exercises appeared to be essential in conducting the feat.

There are inexplicable mysteries in the air we breathe and in the various organs of the body, about which modern science knows nothing. We have learned a little about these air mysteries by the invention of the radio-radar-television mechanism. Previous to these inventions, no one had believed in the air mysteries that we have discovered. We will recover more of these lost and miraculous powers of the body as we resurrect its dormant and deranged organs by living more in harmony with cosmic law.

Carrel says that man is not confined to his body, but diffuses through space. In telepathic phenomena, he instantaneously sends out a part of himself, a sort of emanation, which joins a far-away relative or friend. He thus expands to great distances. He may cross oceans and continents in a time too short to be estimated.

The hypnotist and his subject are sometimes observed to be bound together by an invisible bond, which seems to emanate from the subject. When the communication is established between the hypnotist and his subject the former can, by suggestion from a distance, command the latter to perform certain acts. At this moment, a telepathic relation is established between them. In such an instance, two distant individuals are in contact with each other, yet both appear to be confined within their respective anatomical limits. Thought seems to be transmitted, like electro-magnetic waves, from one region of space to another. We do not know its velocity. Neither biologist, physicists nor astronomers have taken into account the existence of metaphysical phenomena.

Telepathy is a primary datum of observation. We know that Mind is not entirely described within the four dimensions of the physical continuum. It is situated simultaneously within the material Universe and elsewhere. It may insert itself into the cerebral cells and stretch outside space and time, like an alga, which fastens to a rock and lets its tendrils drill out into the mystery of the ocean. We are totally ignorant of the realities that lie outside space and time. We may suppose that a telepathic communication is an encounter, beyond the four dimensions of our universe, between the immaterial parts of two minds. But it is more convenient to consider these phenomena as being produced by the expansion of the individual into space.

In rare instances in the polluted realm of civilization, it still occurs that strange intelligence is shown by a child of perhaps five or six years of age, and the child is regarded as a prodigy. Modern science is unable to offer any sensible explanation of this peculiar phenomena. It may be a case where polluted air has not yet had time to dull and dormantize the spiritual centers in the child's head, and it is able to contact and receive certain phases of Higher Intelligence direct form the Cosmic Source, as the Ancient Masters did ages ago. In a few years, polluted air has done its destructive work, and the child who was once a prodigy, sinks in the realm of intelligence to the level of the social pattern of the masses. Thus do we become what our environment make us, while we in turn make the world in which we live?

Chapter No.6
Spiritual Powers

"We possess no technique capable of penetrating the mysteries of the brain .... Our intelligence can no more realize the immensity of the brain than the extent of the sidereal universe .... The cerebral substance contains more than twelve thousand millions of cells." (Carrel, in *"Man The Unknown,"* pp 9, 95)

The overt admission of the greatest medico-scientist since Darwin and Huxley clearly exposes the falsity of medical claims about solving the secrets of the chemical, physiological, psychological and biological operations of the body, so fearfully and wonderfully made. (Ps. 139:14)

In a lecture delivered at Dornach, Switzerland, April 1, 1922 Rudolf Steiner said: "In his head, in the wonderful convolutions of his brain, man is the image of the entire cosmos. In the body of the mother the human being is formed as an image and likeness of the Universe. Man is first brain, the image of the cosmos. We can study the cosmos by studying the human embryo in its early stages." When Cosmic Radiation starts the formation of a new person, the process begins with the brain, and next with the nerves.

A 26-day old foetus consists almost entirely of brain substance. The body then looks like an elongated brain. The head of a normal, new-born babe is more fully developed than is any other part of the body, and develops less after birth than any other part. This fact indicates the relative importance of the brain.

The brain, spinal cord and nerves are by far the most important parts of the body. These organs are found to be normal in persons who are said to have died of starvation. They are sustained by the oxygen and nitrogen gases in the air and the oxygen and hydrogen gases in the vapor in the air man inhales.

Every part of the body and every organ and gland are under the direction and control of the brain, thru the agency of the nerve system. Without the five physical sense organs and the brain and nerves, man could have no knowledge of the physical world, nor of anything in it. He would not be conscious of his own existence. He could not be aroused from his slumber any more than a tree can become conscious of the animal plane.

Spiritual Intelligence

Spiritual Intelligence is a phenomenon so far beyond the comprehension of modern man, that the very term means nothing to him. One author says that "Radar is the new scientific name applied to a most ancient occult practice."

Birds live in the higher, purer currents of air. Their spiritual intelligence organs have not been crippled by the poison air of civilization, and much of their conduct is inexplicable. They fly in large groups, so in the same direction, perform in various ways, and wheel in the air as if controlled by one Great Mind. That is an example of the work of the Cosmic Mind in cases of animals whose spiritual chambers have not been crippled by poisoned air.

The same delicate powers of electro-magnetism enable

the birds to fly on a curve. These curves are derived from aerial magnetism, of which, so far, man is able to use only the north-pointing vibratory-rays. Man's skull contains the ruined remains of the most perfect radio-radar-television mechanism that one can imagine, with five tubes termed Sinuses, all of them dual purpose, with built-in radio-net antenna, automatic power rectifier and automatic control. This mechanism in man's skull is the original pattern that has been imitated by the work of art. The imitation cannot begin to compare with the original. It is only an artificial replica of what man once had and lost.

Man's brain and nerves are the physical mechanism that releases him from his physical tomb of silence and darkness, and gives him all the knowledge he has of his physical being and physical environment. Before his radio-radar-television mechanism was ruined by poisonous gases, it released him from his physical senses and physical environment, nullified the illusion of space and time and revealed his dual personality, to the effect that he is temporal in the physical and eternal in the spiritual. Then the Spiritual Light of the Cosmos illuminated the Field of Infinitude in man's physical consciousness, and his Spiritual Consciousness, becoming active, made him omniscient for that period. The past and the future, space and time, vanished and became for him the Eternal Present.

In the realm of Spiritual Intelligence, the first new psychic sensation is that of a strange duality in oneself. As this change comes, man finds himself in a world entirely new and unknown to him. It has nothing in common with the physical world. It has no sides nor limits; all is visible at once with at every point. Everything is unified, linked together. Everything is explained by something else, which in its turn explains another thing. To describe the first impressions or sensations, it is necessary to describe all at once. Should one attempt to describe the realm of Spiritual Intelligence, one has no words for that purpose. Language that describes the physical world cannot describe the Spiritual. That is the reason why one who has had mystical experiences uses, for expressing them, those forms of images and words of the physical world. But these describe the physical world not the Spiritual. Therefore, one who returns from the realm of Spiritual Intelligence, the mystical states of consciousness, cannot describe one's experiences because it cannot be done in the language of the physical world, and one know no other.

This is the reason for much of the allegory found in the Bible — eternal truths are explained in the only words physical man can understand.

Man's Intelligence

Man's body is composed of trillions of cells. Each cell is composed of millions of atoms, each of which is a miniature solar system, with "planets" in the form of elections whirling at tremendous speed around a common center of attraction.

The cells of man's body are intelligentized by Cosmic Consciousness, and animatized by Cosmic Force.

Man's intelligence comes through his cells, direct from the Cosmic Source. Cosmic Intelligence is limited in man due to his limited capacity to receive and express it. This capacity arranges men into many classes; and those of each class express intelligence according to the condition of the body. The more perfect the body, the greater the intelligence it will express.

Man is a creature of vibratory impressions received from Cosmic Rays. This makes modern man's capacity of consciousness very small in his present degenerate state. He is dependent upon his five degenerate physical senses to contact the radiations of the Cosmos and these senses are more or less deficient, while the Five Spiritual Senses have been dormantized and rendered useless by the poisoned air of his environment.

Intelligence of Animals

Naturalists tell us that there are perhaps five hundred other senses used by bugs, birds and beasts. Poisoned air has not damaged their sense organs. Ants, bees and caterpillars navigate by the sun or the moon. Their eyes can detect sun-rays even thru clouds. Gymnarchius Niloticus, a fresh water fish, sends out electric impulses at a rate of several hundred a second, which create an electric field — something that degenerated man has difficulty in detecting. This fish feels things at long distances in this manner. Birds of prey that see miles away, do the trick neatly with devices in their eyes that enable them to keep their sight fixed, once they have seen something they want.

Man can do this in reverse by watching an air-plane vanish. He can see it much farther if he keeps his eyes fixed on it.

Flashes of light by fire-flies are code signals by which the males attract the females. Bats make super-sounds to guide them by echoes which few but they can hear. More surprising is the fact that some insects, which bats eat, have the ability to detect the super-sounds and thus escape the bats.

Water beetles that skate on ponds move fast but never collide. Their sensitive legs feel the force of the invisible waves caused by the other skating bugs and that feeling tells them the direction to go to avoid a collision. The dragon-fly's neck is its compass. Its head is large, and any object that changes its course bends its neck. Then receptors in the neck send vibrations to put the bug back on its correct course. Locusts have sensitive spots on their heads that detect any change in the direction of flight.

Following mysterious highways in the sky, migratory birds travel north and south annually. From nesting grounds in the far north, to the south they go for the winter. Birds have done this in North America since the Ice Age, yet science is still uncertain as to how they follow their precise schedules and paths of flight, returning year after year to the same places in the north and south.

Many birds fly tremendous distances, sometimes non-stop, over thousands of miles of open ocean, returning in the spring by entirely different routes. No one yet knows how they navigate.

Small Asiatic birds, migrating between Siberia and India, cross the 20,000 foot peaks of the Himalayan Mountains. The Pacific Golden Plover flies each fall 2,400 miles across an Islandless course from Alaska to Hawaii, finding its destination unerringly. Long-distance champion of the bird world is the Artic Tern. Nesting as far north as there is land, on the islands rimming the Artic Sea, these birds fly in early September across the ocean to Europe, thence down the west coast of Africa, and eventually to the fringes of the Antarctic Ocean, the globetrotting Tern covers a distance of some 22,000 miles in one year.

In the field of television, Deslandres said that the homing-sense of birds appears to rise as the effect of a mysterious electric perception. He wrote: "Birds can home over territory that offers no visible landmarks. I have seen a pigeon released from a balloon at a height of 5,000 feet. The bird was carried in a closed box. As soon as released, it rapidly described two circles round the balloon and then, without hesitation, darted off in the direction of its dove-cote 250 miles away."

Man A Miniature Universe

Paracelsus said: "Man, as microcosm, is formed of the same elements as the Universe, as Macrocosm."

In the Sankhys doctrine concerning the twenty-five elements of Being, we are told that man's five physical senses are only the exteriorized products of the five corresponding latent specializations of the primary ego-forming Conscious Essence or Soul Substance – the Department of Eternal Knowledge.

So the Ancient Masters taught that as man is Microcosm, a miniature Universe, all things contained in the Macrocosm are also contained in the Microcosm in character if not in degree.

The special sense organs in the perfect bodies of the

Ancient Masters were normal and in sympathetic vibration with Cosmic Radiation, hence they could travel in a direct line, as birds now do, toward a distant goal that would be invisible and unknown to modern man. They were able to detect vibrations that our dulled, dormant, degenerated Spiritual Chambers cannot perceive.

Man Is Dead As He Lives

Consider man in a faint, or unconscious from drugs or anesthetics or injury. His body otherwise functions with normal activity to maintain physical life. Nothing is absent but his physical consciousness. The subconscious power, the inner, spiritual man, is intact, uninjured, unchanged, and active. It is only the physical aspect of the conscious mind that is inactive functionless, as a result of which the open eyes can see nothing, the ears can hear nothing, and the physical powers of smelling, tasting and feeling are absent.

With his live physical faculties inactive, closed and shut off from receiving any vibratory impressions conveying intelligence of the physical world, and also being unable to send forth any messages, the conscious mind of physical man is closed and dead to all physical existence.

Such man is literally dead as he lives, so far as his conscious contact with the physical world is concerned.

<u>Chapter No.7</u>
Telepathy

"Thought seems to be transmitted, like electro-magnetic waves, from one region of space to another. It has not been possible so far to measure the speed of telepathic communications. Telepathy is a primary datum of observation. If thought should some day be found to flash through space as light does, our theories about the constitution of the Universe would have to be (greatly) modified." (Alexis Carrel; *"Man The Unknown,"* pp. 261) Telepathy is knowledge. As knowledge is psychic, it must of necessity follow that Telepathy originates in the Psychic Realm.

Telepathy is of two kinds: (1) Physical telepathy that is able to break thru into man's physical consciousness and there find interpretation in the physical channels of intelligence; and (2) Psychic Telepathy, which never enters the physical mind of man and is interpreted solely by psychic laws. Physical telepathy is confined entirely in thoughts, feelings, events and history of man's existence in the physical body.

Psychic telepathy is confined wholly to the knowledge of Eternity in all its stages from near to far; to the present as it exists in the Psychic World; and to the future as it exists in the Cosmic Mind. Physical telepathy is the product of Cosmic Mind insofar as it relates to the physical body.

Physical telepathy is the passage into man's conscious mind of knowledge from Cosmic Mind. It often brings facts of tremendous weight; and still more often it brings mere moods, thoughts, feelings and the happiness of life. What it brings is entirely applicable to the needs or associations of the physical body. Psychic telepathy originates in the Psychic or Cosmic Mind, and includes knowledge that relates to spiritual life, or the existence of the spiritual body.

Such knowledge cannot be interpreted by the physical mind that is not trained, and can be understood only by psychic laws. Reason, logic and the mental processes of man's physical mind are useful only in the physical mind. They do not apply to Cosmic Mind. He who declares that he will accept only what his reason tells him is true, will never know aught of truth lying beyond his physical faculties. Man's reason is ruled by physical laws, by what he is taught, and the knowledge of modern science is limited to physical faculties and mechanical inventions.

Physical man believes that which he sees, feels, smells, and tastes, and has faith in the deductions drawn by his conscious mind. But all these are parts of his physical existence only, and have almost nothing to do with that real knowledge which must come from another source and be interpreted by laws different from those he employs and is taught to use in physical life.

Psychic telepathy is knowledge that comes to the Psychic Mind, as revealed to man by the spirit in him. That knowledge has relation wholly to things, facts, events, plans, thoughts and purposes that are part of Universal Life, and man is conscious of such knowledge only in the Spirit. To be able to interpret that higher knowledge, one must be taught to think irrationally and without physical facts. (I Cor. 2:9-11)

Sir F. H. Myers, of the English Society' of Psychic Research, was convinced that man possessed a second mind. He wrote: "Ordinary consciousness makes up but a small part of man's personality. Beneath the threshold of this working consciousness there lies, not merely an unconscious complex of organic processes, but an intelligent vital control. The subliminal consciousness is evoked by suggestion, which is able to tap the deeper stratum of being, which is more independent of passing impressions and environment than is the ordinary stratum of consciousness." — Cosmic Mind, p. 72.

"Ordinary consciousness" and "working consciousness" mean the physical mind. "Passing impressions and environment" mean the physical mind. "Unconscious complex of organic processes" is a synonym for Cosmic Mind. "Intelligent vital control" is a synonym for Cosmic Mind. So also is the "subliminal consciousness" and "the deeper stratum of being."

A simpler translation of this scientific phraseology is to say, the Psychic Mind is not conscious in the sense of the physical (working) mind is conscious, but it includes all there is of living existence, has deep vital control of everything, in supreme intelligence, and is higher than the physical being.

There is a tendency of those who have discovered the existence of the Psychic Mind, to take flights into the ether and pass into mysticism. True mysticism is helpful in the discovery of hidden knowledge, but the spurious usually encountered in this field is a fraud. The physical mind is man's working, physical intelligence. That is its scope of duty, and that duty it performs – subject to the habits, cravings and cries of the physical body.

The physical mind is greatly limited. Because it is ignorant of the nature of the power in the cell of protoplasm that animates it, or what is beyond the earth in the Universe, the physical mind fabricates and formulates mystic explanations and leaps into abysses of speculation which, in time, warp the intelligence.

Many persons, says Carrel, are shackled by mental chains of their own making. They refuse to look beyond the limit of what they are taught or what they believe. Their mind is closed.

Carrel says that man diffuses through space in a positive way. In telepathic phenomena, he instantaneously sends out part of himself, a sort of emanation, which joins a far-away friend or relative, as God joins mankind all over the world.

Man thus expands too great distances. He may cross continents and oceans in a space of time too short to be estimated, as the flashing of the mind. He is capable of finding in the midst of a crowd the person whom he must meet. Those endowed with this form of activity behave like extensible beings, amebas of a strange kind, capable of sending pseudopods to prodigious distances. Van David declared that his experiences in India left in his mind not the slightest doubt as to the actuality of telepathic communications. Numerous experiments have been conducted in telepathy, and the fact of thought-transference has been definitely established. The hypnotist and his subject are sometimes observed to be linked together by a spiritual bond that seems to emanate from the subject. When communication is established between them, the hypnotist can, by suggestion from a distance, command the subject to perform certain acts. At that moment, telepathic relation is established between them, and two distant persons are in contact with each other, although both appear to be confined within their respective anatomical limits.

Luther Burbank, plant wizard of Santa Rosa, Calif., told in Hearst's International Magazine of June 1923, how he, his sister and his mother practiced telepathy for decades, but had previously told no one of the secret because he did not desire to be considered supernatural or a liar – another reason why persons shackled themselves with mental chains of their own making.

Burbank wrote: "I believe we have all been broadcasting and receiving from the beginning of human thought. Those who can send messages to particular persons differ from others only in that they can direct their thought waves to where they wish them to go. Thoughts are produced by discharges of electric force. So are radio messages. The two things are the same, except that the human machine is infinitely more wonderful and capable of incomparably greater achievements."

Soon after his arrival in California, Burbank received a telepathic request for information from a friend in Massachusetts. He returned the answer by telepathy and a few days later received confirmation of the phenomenon. He said that in the declining years of his mother's life, he often summoned his sister telepathically to Santa Rosa, and she invariably arrived on the next train. We know that Mind is not described within the four dimensions of the physical continuum. It is situated simultaneously within the material

Universe and elsewhere. It may insert itself into the cerebral cells and stretch outside space and time. We are utterly ignorant of the realities that lie outside space and time. We may suppose that telepathic communication is an encounter, beyond the four dimensions of our Universe, between the immaterial parts of two Minds.

To an all-seeing Mind there is no veil, no curtain, no darkness, no obscurity, no denial, no hiding, no surprise, no doubts, nothing that is not plain, certain and understandable.

Two propositions are all that are necessary to cover the whole field of physical existence: 1. The physical body is seriously handicapped by the physical consciousness. It is struggling with its vital burden, and it employs the ordinary physical mind to do its intelligent labor. This is the working consciousness that is fed by the five physical senses. 2. There are countless things, events, conditions and purposes that the ordinary physical mind is unable to grasp because these cannot enter through the channels of the ordinary physical senses. But they may be clearly seen in the mind, being understood by the things that are made visible. (Rom. 1:20) The Psychic Mind know all, never falters, never misleads.

Having learned of the existence of the Psychic Mind, the rest is not difficult. There are methods by which it may be possible to "tap this deeper stratum of our being" and secure some of its precious knowledge. This must be done in practical ways, and not under the name of some peculiarism, Christian Science, theosophy, or other spurious claims to supernaturalism advanced by sordid institutions that live and thrive on human ignorance.

These institutions are fixed and organized; they have their

limitations and beyond that line the members and teachers are not allowed to go. Mankind is in need of a sensible period, with all oppression, suppression and mental limitations banished, including fantastic creeds, suppressive dogmas, and false beliefs that have grown up out of ignorance, darkness and miseducation.

When people open their minds, when they really search for truth and can be reached with the facts as they are, as entirely natural, plain, and free of all mysterious and misleading trimmings, the civilized world will be born anew into the realm of Science of the Ancient Masters. For the long night that has hung over civilization since despots drove the Masters underground, will then pass into the Golden Dawn of a Glorious Day.

Chapter No.8
Television (A)

Our ignorance (of man) is profound. Most of the questions put to them who study human beings remain without answer. Immense regions of our inner world (body) are still unknown. We lack almost entirely a knowledge of the physiology of the nerve cells (p.4.) We possess no technique capable of penetrating the mysteries of the brain (p. 9.) Our intelligence can no more realize the immensity of the brain than the extent of the sidereal universe (p. 95.) – *Man, The Unknown,* 1935, by Dr. Alexis Carrel, expert anatomist and physiologist.

Man is what his brain makes him. The difference in men is the difference in brain development and function. That marks the difference between sage and serf. In Sanskrit writings the Pineal Gland in the brain is listed as the Seventh Nerve Ganglion. Around that gland is woven a very strange story. It is said that the Masters considered this gland to be the seat of the Soul. As modern science claims that man has no Soul, of course it needs no seat.

Modern anatomists assert that the gland is the vestige of an organ of sense, presumably of sight, and they term it "the unpaired eye." Thus we learn how little modern science actually knows about the body and its glands and organs.

This particular gland, now seriously atrophied and apparently useless in modern man, is esoterically known as the Third Eye, or the Spiritual Eye of the Seer. It is said to be the organ of Television, and so functioned when developed and activated by the vivifying force of the Serpentine Fire.

This force of many names, termed also as Speirema or Paraklete in ancient symbology, is the most mysterious force in the body. Its situs appears to be in the sacral plexus, and, in Sanskrit writings, it was called the Kundalini. It is something about which little is known except by occult science.

In a word, the higher functions of the human body are above the plane of Materialism. When we rise above that plane, we pass beyond the scope and range of modern science. For it refuses to investigate the psychic Phenomena of Life. So these higher functions of the body are a mystery to modem science. They are known only to occultism, and are seldom made public.

The spinal cord extends from the brain down to the sacral plexus – and that much modem science knows. Along this high-tension transmission line the Force of Creation, the Sacred Fire generated in the Tree of Life (Gen. 2:9) may be diverted from the animalistic productive centers of the physical plane and directed up the Silver (spinal) Cord to the high Intellective Centers of Spirituality in the Golden Bowl (Brain) (Eccl. 12:6.)

In its upward movement through the spinal cord of the body, this spiritual consciousness stops at Seven Shrines to activate their functions. The Book with Seven Seals represents the Body and its Seven Shrines (Rev. 5.) The buds on the rod of Aaron are symbols of these Shrines (Num. 17:8.) The opening of the Seven Seals literally means the activation of the force of the Seven Shrines, Chakras, ganglionic nerve centers, of the Spinal Cord, and the unfolding of Spiritual Consciousness within. The Spiritual

Consciousness passing upward through the Spinal Cord increases as these Seven Centers become more active.

When the lower principles govern man, he is not attuned to his own higher Self, and his vibrations do not harmonize with those of the higher plane. The Spiritual Consciousness in man blossoms forth in the brain when fed by the Spiritual Essence of Creation generated in the Tree of Life. This force raises him up, in the third Resurrection, from the earthly plane of productive animalism to the higher plane of Spiritual Intellectualism. That is Spiritual Consciousness termed the Kundalini by the Masters. It makes man a Seer instead of a server.

Three thousand years ago Hindu doctors were grinding the dried Generative Glands into powder and administering it to their patients in the hope of restoring youth and vigor. They know that dynamic vitality owes most of its power to the Life Essence produced by the Glands of the Creative Force.

It is logical to understand that a creative force in man so potent that it produces New Life and performs creative work on the physical plane of production, will work surprising wonders in the Intellective Centers of those who conserve it and direct it to that use. The religious fanatics of the "dark ages" who were not properly informed on this important subject, submitted to emasculation in order to free themselves from the temptation of concupiscence, and thereby lost the precious power they had sought to save. In the Bible these men are said to have been made eunuchs for the kingdom of heaven's sake (Mat. 19:12.) That statement was interpolated in the gospels sometime subsequent to 325 A.D. Succinctly, the seven grades of Being represented in the human microcosm and recognized in occult science, are divided into two primal departments, the lower and the higher.

The four lower, technically denominated the "Quarternary," are (1) physical body, (2) etheric double, (3) subtil or astral vehicle, and (4) concrete mentality. The three higher, the "Ternary" or "Triad," are (5) higher or abstract intellect, (6) intuition, and (7) pure ego. The latter three are noumenal and immortal. It is this super-phenomenal Triad that is symbolized in ancient religions by the Sun, the Father of all; and the allegorical journey to the Sun is a symbolic designation of rendering fully actual and latent potentialities of these three transcendent microcosmic principles, as we have explained in our work titled *The Ancient Sun God*.

This higher goal corresponds to the King's chamber in the Great Pyramid, and when attained in physical life, it is the result of the concomittant activation of the two strange cerebral glands, the Pineal, which Descartes identified as the point of contact between Brain and Soul, and the Pituitary. When this activation occurred, it was termed the Marriage of the Lamb, as we have explained in *The Magic Wand* (Rev. 19:7.)

It is well to state here that when the Pituitary is stimulated by the rising Serpentine Fire from the Tree of Life, it glows with a faint roseate hue, and rippling rings of bluish light flow from it which, if the stimulation is continued, gradually grow greater, extending upward thru the third ventricle of the brain, illuminating the interior of the ventricles, and "approaching ever closer to the sleeping eye of Shiva" (dormant Peneal.)

"Under the benign heat and radiance of the electric fire of the Pituitary, the Single Eye of the Masters (Mat. 6:22) thrills, flickers, and finally opens." The term "open" meaning that the gland goes into action.

Thus the mystic journey to the Moon was equated with the consummation of man's psycho-mental development, and the consequent psychic actuation of the Pituitary gland; and the allegoric journey thence to the Sun with the activation of the Pineal, involving noumenal illumination; and the "sparking" process between the Pituitary (female) and Pineal (male) glands with the Hermetic Marriage of the Sun and Moon, of Hermes and Aphrodite, or of Osiris and Isis, — all names meaning the same thing.

Chapter No.9
Television (B)

In the spiritual realm of television, Deslandres declared that the homing-sense of birds appears to arise as the effect of some kind of electric perception. He wrote: "I have seen a pigeon released from a balloon at a height of 5,000 feet. The bird was carried in a closed box. As soon as released, it rapidly made to circles around the balloon and then, without hesitation, darted of in the direction of its dovecot 250 miles away."

It has been established that birds can home over territory that offers no visible landmarks. Vultures appear to possess telepathic powers. If only one appears in sight and discovers a carcass from its dizzy heights, within a short time many of them will have assembled round the feast from points as far as 50 to 100 miles or more. Kant had recorded the incident of how Swedenborg, famous Swedish chemist and mystic, was greatly perturbed on a certain occasion by the outbreak of a fire near his own home in Stockholm, 200 miles away from where he then was, and could not be quieted by friends at a dinner party. He became calm of his own accord in about an hour, informing those present that the fire had been extinguished, but dangerously near his home. The description he then gave of the conflagration was verified by the first post from Stockholm.

A remarkable example of spiritual vision appears in the case of Apollonius of Tyana, who came in time to be presented to the world as the Jesus of the gospels, and the

Paul of the Epistles, and the John of Revelation. But that is another story, and a highly important and interesting one, and any who desire to read it will find it in that work titled *"Awaken the World Within."*

Domitian, the Roman Emperor and a bloody tyrant, who had sentenced to death his own cousin and nephew by marriage, Flavius Clements, was assassinated in 96 A.D. by one Stephanus, a freed-man of Clements, who stabbed Domitian to death in his bedroom. Although the deed was done in Rome, Apollonius was a witness of it in Ephesus, many miles away, according to Philostratus in his *"Life of Apollonius."* He reported the event as follows: "About midday Apollonius was delivering an address on philosophy in Ephesus at 'the moment when Domitian was assassinated in Rome.' Stopping suddenly in his lecture, he first lowered his voice, as if he were terrified, and then, though with less vigor than was usual with him, he continued his exposition, as one who between his words caught glimpses of something foreign to his subject, and at last he lapsed into silence, as one who had been interrupted in his discourse.

"Then with an awful glance at the ground, and stepping forward three or four paces from his pulpit, he cried: "Courage, Stephaus; smite the tyrant, smite him," – not as one who derives from some looking-glass a faint image of the truth, but as one who sees things with his own eyes, and is taking part in the tragedy.

"All Ephesus was at his lecture, and the multitude was struck dumb with astonishment; but Apollonius, pausing as those who are trying to see and wait until their doubts are ended, said, 'Take heart, gentlemen, for the tyrant has today been slain; and why do I say today? The very moment in which I kept silent, he suffered for his crimes.'

"The people of Ephesus thought that this was a fit of madness on his part; and although they were anxious that it should be true, yet they were anxious about the risk they ran in giving ear to his words, whereupon he said: "I am not surprised at those who do not yet accept my story, for not even all Rome as yet is cognizant of it. But behold, Rome begins to know it; for the rumor runs this way and that, and thousands are now convinced of it; and they begin to leap for joy, twice as many as before, and trice as many as they, and four times as many, yea the whole of the populace there. And this news will travel thither also; and although I would have defer your celebration in honor thereof to the fitting season, when you will receive this news.'

"They were still skeptical, when swift runners arrived with the good news, and bore testimony to the sage's wisdom; for the tyrant's death, and the day that brought the event to birth, the hour of midday and the murderer to whom he addressed his exhortation, — everything agreed with the revelation which the spirit had made to Apollonius in the midst of his harangue.

"Thirty days later Nerva sent a letter to Apollonius, saying that he was already in possession of the Empire of the Romans, thanks to the good-will of the gods and to his good counsels; and he added that he would more easily retain it if Apollonius would come to advise him" (pp. 394-5.)

The student is admonished to keep in mind this remarkable man, born February 16, A.D. 2, of wealthy parents. For a man so influential, so prominent and so wise as to be invited to act as councillor to the Emperor of the great Roman Empire, was certainly worthy of being especially considered and honored by a later Emperor, and he was in a most glorious way.

In 325 A.D. the First Council of Nicaea was called by Constantine the Great, for the purpose of establishing a new religious system to supersede the very ancient system of the Lemurian Masters, because its principles hampered the work of despots by enlightening the people.

The world little suspects that it gets new religious systems in practically the same way that it gets new political systems; and the people have no alternative but to accept what the rulers and leaders select and prepare for them. And so at this convention of bishops, two hundred twenty-five years after his death, Apollonius, the greatest philosopher and mystic of the first century, was chosen by a vote of the bishops to be and became the gospel Jesus. That is the way the great man of the New Testament came into being, and the purpose of the New Testament was to present him formally to the world as "the savior of mankind."

It required many years, millions of dollars and millions of murders to force this new god upon the populace of the Roman Empire; but the job was done, and done so well that millions of so-called Christians are still afraid to ask or investigate as to whether their "savior" was actually a man or only a fictitious character, like Santa Claus.

When the gospel compiler put into the mouth of the gospel Jesus the words "I will come again" (Jn. 14:3, 28,) he made a statement that is literally a mixture of truth and fiction, just as practically all statements in the Bible are.

The Lamb of God

Christ's Second Coming is based on this statement which the writers of the New Testament put into the mouth of their hero: "In my Father's house are many mansions; if it were not so, 1 would have told you, 1 will come again, and receive you unto myself; that where 1 am, there ye may be also" (Jn. 14:2, 3.)

In this particular instance we are dealing with the symbolism of the Zodiac, the ancient Wheel of Life. The "many mansions" in my Father's house are the twelve houses of the Zodiac. The gospel Jesus here represents the head sign of the Zodiac, — Aries, Ram, old Lamb, — the Lamb of God (Jn. 1:36.)

When Jesus has twelve apostles, he represents the Sun, and the apostles represent the twelve "mansions" of the Zodiac. But when he is the head sign of the Zodiac, he has only eleven apostles. One had to be disposed of to make a place for him, — and see how skillfully the church fathers got rid of Judas, all of which is understood by the exoteric.

Christ's second coming is based on the Great Circuit of the Earth, which it makes as it passes through the range of a Constellation, represented by a cycle of 2,160 years. In each Grand Cycle of 25,920 years the Earth passes through all Twelve Mansions of the Zodiac.

And so this means that every 25,920 years, this Christ (Aries) comes, and reigns each time for 2,160 years. Thus the biblical statement is true when properly presented.

Chapter No.10
The Fourth Dimension (A)

We look not at the things that are seen, but at the things that are not seen: for the things seen are temporal; but the things not seen are eternal. For the invisible things of Him from the creation of the world are clearly seen (in the mind,) being understood (mentally) by the things that are made (visible.) (Rom. 1:20; 2 Cor. 4:18.) The Masters divided the world into the visible and the invisible, and taught the neophyte that the invisible could be known by a clear understanding of the visible. That knowledge was lost when the Ancient Wisdom was destroyed.

In all the history of human thought, people have always divided the world into the visible and the invisible. They have always taught that the visible world, accessible to their direct observation, represents something very small, something perhaps even non-existent, an optical illusion, in comparison with the vast invisible world. The theory of the existence of hidden knowledge, surpassing all the knowledge that a man can attain in schools and colleges, has always prevailed, and increases in men's minds by their realization of the insolubility of many problems confronting them. Scientist may deceive themselves, and think that their knowledge increases, that they understand more than they knew before. But sometimes they may be sincere with themselves and admit that in relation to the fundamental problems of existence, they are as helpless as a child, although they have invented many clever instruments that have complicated life, but have not rendered it any more comprehensible. The invisible world is the world of small quantities and also of large quantities.

The invisible world is the world of micro-organisms, cells; the microscopic and the ultra-microscopic world; and still further, it is the world of molecules, atoms, electrons and vibrations. Then again it is the world of invisible stars, other solar systems, unknown parts of the Universe. The visible world disappears from sight no matter which way we go.

So far as we know, on all levels of the common man's development, he has always found that the causes of visible phenomena lie beyond the range of his ordinary observation.

Man has found that among observable phenomena, certain facts could be regarded as causes of other facts. But such deductions were insufficient for this explanation of everything that occurred around him and within his own body. To be able to explain the causes, it was necessary to have an invisible world consisting of spirits or vibrations, or both.

The principle problem which attracted man's attention by its insolubility and which, by the form of its approximate solution determined the direction and development of human thought, was and still is the problem of Death.

Man could not reconcile himself to the theory of death as annihilation. Too many things contradicted it. There were to many traces of the dead, their faces, words, opinions, promises, threats, and the feeling which they engendered — fear, jealousy, desire, etc. All these continued to live in him, and the fact of the death of these people was more and more forgotten.

Man saw his dead friend or foe in his dreams, appearing exactly as before. He evidently existed somewhere and could come from there at will. Furthermore, modern religious teachings fail to satisfy thinking people. There is always a more ancient system of popular belief back of it, upon which the modern system is based. Behind Christianity stands the ancient religion and the scriptures of that religion. Thinking men speculate on whether Christianity is but a modified form of some ancient religion, with the basic principles and doctrines omitted, modified, or replaced by untenable dogmas, designed to put into the hands of the rulers and leaders more power over the people.

It appears inconsistent to a thinking man for Christianity to use the scriptures of the ancients, and at the same time condemn the authors of those scriptures and their system of worship.

For instance, Christianity uses the scriptures of the so-called pagans, then condemns them as a group of heathenish idolaters. This course is not only highly inconsistent, but it emits an odor that is highly offensive and obnoxious. This speculation increases when the fact is known that history shows it was urgently necessary for the Roman rulers to crush the ancient religion and its worshippers with the Roman army, and to force the people by punishment, torture, and even death, to accept the new system now termed Christianity. It is not regular nor proper to go to such extremes to persuade man to accept that which is better than what he has. When we show a man that he is traveling the wrong trail to reach the goal of his great desire, it is never necessary to punish and otherwise torture him to persuade him to change his course and join us on the path that leads to the glorious life of eternal bliss. The fact that this was done, and done on an enormous scale as history shows, is the strongest evidence a reasonable person could demand to convince him that he is the victim of a plot that was not planned for his protection.

It has been clearly evident for ages that if the problem of death aid the future life can be approached in any way, it must be done by a very different method than that contained in Christian dogmas. Until he has a definite answer, one way or the other, to the question of the invisible world and life after death, man cannot think of anything else without creating a whole series of contradictions. Right or wrong, man must find for himself some kind of an explanation that will satisfy him and harmonize with the laws of the Universe. He must base his consideration of the problem of death and the future life upon either science, or philosophy, or religion.

The "scientific" denial of the possibility of life after death, and the pseudo-religious assertion of future life for those who accept a certain faith, while damnation shall be the fate of those who fail to accept that faith (Mk. 16:16) leaves a thinking man far from being satisfied and contented.

Physical science know nothing of the world beyond the grave, and its ethics forbid it to investigate the spiritual world under that definition. Pseudo-religion (for we have no other kind now) creates the other world in the image of the earthly world, and its god in the image of the earthly man. This unsatisfactory situation, this helplessness of man, in the face of the problems of the invisible world and of death, becomes particularly obvious when we realize that the Universe is much larger and more complex than we had hitherto believed, and that what we think we know, occupies but a very small place amidst that which we know not.

Physical science has shown by investigation and demonstration that we cannot trust the eyes with what we see, nor the hands with what we feel. The real world eludes all such attempts to ascertain its existence and its character. The idea of the Fourth Dimension, and the theories of many dimensional space, show the way by which we may expand the knowledge of ourselves and of the universe.

The Fourth Dimension is an expression often encountered in

conversational language and in literature. But it is seldom that any one has a clear conception of what it means. The Fourth Dimension is generally used as the synonym of the mysterious, miraculous, supernatural, incomprehensible, and incognizable – as a kind of general definition of the phenomena of the super-physical world. Modern spiritualists and occultists often use this expression in their literature, assigning to the realm of the Fourth Dimension all the phenomena of the invisible or astral world. But they fail to explain what the term means. From what they say, one can understand only that the chief quality which then ascribed to the Fourth Dimension is "unknowableness."

The connecting of the idea of the Fourth Dimension with existing theories of the invisible world is quite fantastic. For all religious, spiritualistic, theosophic and other theories of the invisible world make it, first of all, exactly similar to the visible and, consequently, a three-dimensional world.

The idea of the Fourth Dimension must have arisen in connection with mathematics, or with the idea of measuring the world. It must have arisen from the theory that, besides the three known dimensions of space (length, breadth and height,) there must also be a Fourth Dimension, inaccessible to our physical perception.

The opinion is sometimes offered that mathematicians know something of the Fourth Dimension that is inaccessible to the common man. Sometimes it is said that one can even find such assertions in literature, that Labatchevsky "discovered" the Fourth Dimension. During the last quarter of a century the discovery of the Fourth Dimension has often been ascribed to Einstein or Minkovsky. After reviewing the various theories concerning the Fourth Dimension, we have no grounds for looking for it anywhere else except in the domain of

Spiritualism.

Chapter No.11
The Fourth Dimension (B)

The great scientist Alexis Carrel, who kept alive for 27 years a heart fragment from a chick embryo, wrote: "Man is made up of a process of phantoms, in the midst of which there strides an unknowable Reality" (*Man The Unknown*, p. 4.)

The chemist analyzes a grain of wheat. He heats another grain and examines it. No difference appears in the two grains. But a peculiar change has occurred. The unheated grain contains an element that the heated grain has lost. The heated grain, if planted, decays in the ground; but the unheated grain, when planted, sprouts and grows and reproduces itself.

Naturalists employ this fact as evidence to prove that cooked and heated substances are dead and unfit for consumption as food.

A living cell and a dead cell are equal in length, breadth and height. In appearance they are exactly alike. But there is a strange element in the living cell that is lacking in the dead cell — something that we are unable to analyze, measure or define.

Physical science terms that element Vital Force, and tries to explain it as a "mode of motion." But the explanation explains nothing. It simply gives a name to a phenomenon that remains inexplicable. Physical science holds that Vital Force is resolvable into physicochemical elements; into simper energy. These theories cannot explain how the one passes into the other, nor in what relation the one stands to the other.

Physical science is unable to express in a physico-chemical formula the simplest manifestation of what it terms "life energy." As long as it cannot do so, it has no authority whatever to regard vital processes as identical with physico-chemical processes.

If physical science possessed any definite knowledge of the unity of vital and physico-chemical phenomena, it could create living bodies. Mechanics make machines much more complicated externally than a simple one-cell organism. But they cannot endow their machines with life, nor make the simplest living creature. This well-known fact proves that there is an unknown and an unmeasurable element in a living organism that is net in a lifeless machine.

Physical science considers three classes of phenomena, to-wit: mechanical, vital and psychic energy. According to its theories, these pass one into another only partially, and apparently without any fixed or calculable proportions.

Consequently, scientists will be justified in explaining vital and psychic processes as a "mode of motion" ONLY when they have devised means of transforming motion into vital and psychic energy and vice versa, and of calculating such transformation.

This means several things that physical science is unable to do. It means that such an affirmation will be possible only when it is shown what number of calories contained in a certain amount of coal is necessary to state the life of one cell; or how many atmospheres of pressure are necessary for the formation of one thought or one logical deduction.

As long as these things remain unknown to physical science, then physical science, as it studies physical, physiological, psychic and biologic phenomena, will regard these as occurring on different planes. Their unity may be presumed, but nothing positively can be affirmed. It is a fact of common observation and demonstration, that in a living man there is an element equally inexplicable and unmeasurable. Which part of man is larger, the measurable or the unmeasurable part?

That unknown, unmeasurable part of man is termed the Fourth Dimension. That term indicates Unconditioned Reality, Absolution, and was symbolized by the Masters with the Undivided Circle, representing Eternity.

We cannot describe the Fourth Dimension as we have no explicable dimension in that direction. We cannot measure everything in man. Two principle properties of Man, Life and Thought, are in the domain of the unmeasurable.

Hall asserts that each of the kingdoms of Nature develops one of the dimensions, and gives the relationships as follows: *Mineral, functions to no dimension — Plant, functions to one dimension — Animal, functions to two dimensions — Man, functions to three dimensions — God, functions to four dimensions.*

Hall continue: "We are told that the Fourth Dimension can be found by dividing a cube into six pyramids so that each of the six surfaces of the cube becomes the base of one of the pyramids. The six pyramids each face the center of the cube, and their six points meet in the exact center. Now, if you can imagine yourself standing in the center where the points meet, looking at all six pyramids at once, you would then be looking at the cube with the fourth dimensional sense" (Super Faculties, p. 40-1.)

We moderns know so little about the mystery of Man, "The Unknown" as Carrel terms him, and his body contains so much that is enigmatical and incomprehensible from the viewpoint of the geometry of three dimensions, that we have no reason to deny the Fourth Dimension in denying "spirits." On the contrary, we have good grounds to look in Man himself for the Fourth Dimension, as the Masters stated (Lu. 17:21.)

Man is an enigma, and the Fourth Dimension promises to

explain something of the enigma. A line is called the first dimension. An extension of lines makes a plane, called the second dimension. An extension of planes makes a solid or cube, called the third dimension. As Man has length, breadth and height, he is physically in the realm of the third dimension.

The mind of most men is limited to three dimensional concepts. This is so in the case of orthodox physical scientists. They consider man as a three dimensional entity and refuse to believe that he is a four-dimensional being. He is only three dimensional, a machine that operates on mechanical energy.

The facts of the Living World that we must consider to reach correct conclusions, are four-dimensional facts that lie beyond the range of physical science. The Ancient Masters used the Circle as a symbol to represent the Fourth Dimension. They taught the neophyte that it contains all things, as Clear Light contains all colors. *To the Masters, the Fourth Dimension was Absolutism. In Absolutism there are no divisions, no opposites, no positive and negative, no male and female, no time and space, no birth and death — no phase of manifestation.*

Law does not exist in the Fourth Dimension. For no law appears in operation until needed; and no phase of law is necessary until the Unit is divided, differentiated, condition.

It is the division of the Unit that produces Duality, and this gives birth to the Primary Law (Polarity,) to which man, in darkness and confusion, has given many and various names.

Chapter No.12
The Fourth Dimension (C)

And I saw a new heaven and a new earth; for the first heaven and the first earth were passed away; and there was no more sea — Then form his effulgent throne the Logos-Sun declared, Behold, I make all things new. — Rev. 21:1,5.

The Apocalyptic Universe is Man, the lesser cosmos, of whom the Logos-Sun is the Architect and Builder, and whom the Sun, Moon and all the Stars of heaven have helped to mould and make: For in every man, however fallen or degraded, are stored up all the forces, both cosmic and deific, which brought him into being. In the Fourth Dimension, in an invisible state, appears that substance of which all things are composed, both spiritual and physical. It is the substance from which the visible world is transformed, not created.

When transformation occurs, the products present the third dimension upon physical examination. But the Fourth Dimension is comprehended by the unorthodox few who can understand, by the things made visible, the properties and qualities of the invisible and the unseen. (Rom.-1:20.)

Invisible substance presents no properties by which it may be known to our physical senses. But it may be understood as we reason from the seen to the unseen, and thus realize that the Visible represents the Invisible.

To our five senses (physical,) invisible substance seems to have no qualities to indicate what we term Matter. Like the air, it seems to have no weight, no mass, no existence. It emits no vibrations that affect our five physical senses. Here is the paradox of all things being contained in what appears as nothing.

That fact passes beyond the comprehension of physical science.

For three centuries the physical scientists postulated the Universe as a dead machine, and believed in the absolute void of celestial space. To "save face" and protect reputation, modern science dares not repudiate the many false theories of the "authorities" that grew out of that erroneous conception, which theories now fill its textbooks with erroneous conclusions.

The illusions arise from the five physical sense organs. Physical science observes the rule that nothing worth while exists beyond the range of man's five physical senses, and the microscope and telescope. That rule has been exploded by the discovery that all visible substance is condensed invisible substance.

The human body is so constituted that it may exist in a tremendous air pressure of 14.7 pounds per square inch and not be conscious of it. Also, it is so constituted that it may exist in the Fourth Dimension, the Spiritual World, and yet not be conscious of that fact. But to him who has attained the Cosmic Consciousness and realizes these things, there is Eternal Life and Eternal Knowledge.

So far as his five physical senses are concerned, man has no knowledge of atmospheric weight and pressure. At sea-level that pressure is 14.7 pounds per square inch. A man of average size supports with his body a tremendous pressure of 38,570 pounds — equal to a solid cube of lead four feet high. But man's body is so constituted that he lives in comfort under this condition, and is totally unconscious of that weight and pressure. When informed of it, he raises his eyebrows in astonishment.

As the physical body cannot detect atmospheric pressure because of a lack of noticeable vibrations, so the physical eye can detect no objects from which it receives no noticeable vibrations. The same philosophy applies to the ear and the surface of the body. We thus observe that, according to the findings of physical science, man could actually be living in the spiritual world now, and yet be totally unconscious of it.

That fact was common knowledge before the Flood. But the appearance of despots at a later time made it necessary for the Masters to conceal their Science in order to preserve it; and the knowledge was finally lost to the multitude. Another case of Lost Wisdom. Then appeared organized systems of religion, of a spurious character, that had no other design but to control the masses. That made it necessary to control the Mind of the masses.

We must control the Mind in order to enslave the Man.

The subconscious mind dwells in the Fourth Dimension. Through hypnosis, it appears to be separated from the body or conscious mind. The hypnotized subject can treat of questions foreign to his conscious knowledge, or reply to questions unknown to him while awake. He can feel the thought and not the word symbol of what a person, near or far away, is thinking; and he can transport his spirit to a distance and describe scenes and events of which he knows nothing when not hypnotized.

That is an example of Eternal Knowledge in operation on the physical plane, and concerning which physical science is silent.

The Masters termed this phenomenon "the release of the soul" from its physical temple, or the "practice of dying." It does not seem natural nor logical that man should suffer somatic death in order to enter the realm of Eternal Knowledge.

Socrates said, *"The great consummation of all philosophy is Death; and he who pursues philosophy aright, is studying how to die"* (Pike, p. 393.) It may be more proper to say that he is acquiring knowledge of the Future Life.

Ages upon ages of mind control has reduced man so low in his state of consciousness, that he has finally lost all contact with the spiritual world, except in rare instances; and it is dangerous for those few persons to publish what they know of the spiritual world. Each cubic foot of air at the earth's surface, which air physical science has declared for three hundred years was void and empty, contains over a trillion trillions of molecules, and they are actually spiritual substance in vibration. That is more particles than there are grains of sand on any desert on earth.

More astonishing, each molecule is composed of atoms, and each atom is a miniature solar system, in which electrons are whirling at terrific speed. Even these amazing facts can hardly give one a fair inkling of the wonders and vastness of the invisible part of the Universe — the Fourth Dimension.

The theory of Evolution had its birth in the idea that so-called Matter was something that actually existed free of the Spirit, and that the Spirit was only a myth of the ancient heathens.

The Evolutionist assumed that Matter had a beginning, and contained in itself all the necessary properties of its existence, including a "desire to progress," and more preposterous, that man was "the product of that progression."

Matter has no beginning. There can be no beginning without an end; for the end is the point of beginning. There must be an end or there can be no beginning. A circle has no beginning because it has no end. That is the reason why the Masters used the O to symbolize Eternity. As Eternity has no beginning, so it has no end.

Physical science is in its first primary lesson of condensing or materializing air. For countless ages the lowly spider has performed that miracle without the necessity of attending a school of chemistry. The intelligence necessary to perform that feat is inherent in the atoms composing the spider's body. The atoms know what to do and how to do it. The modus operandi by which the spider forms its web from the air it inhales is the despair of science. The wisdom of the wasp, the spider, ant and the bee strikes dumb the protagonists of the theory of evolution.

Chapter No.13
Temperance (Time)

In our work titled *"The Mysterious Sphinx"* we referred to the Tarot and included several of the cards, with comment explaining their symbolism. We return to the Tarot and draw out card 14.

I saw a Winged Angel, with the sign of the Sun upon his forehead, and on his breast the square, and within it the triangle, — the sign of the Sacred Book of the Tarot. On his brow was the sign of Eternity and Life, — the Circle. I speak of him in the masculine sense, but the figure is neither male nor female.

In his hands the Angel held two cups — one of gold and one of silver, and between the cups there flowed the incessant stream of Life. His one foot upon the earth and the other upon the sea, was illustrative of the nature of the stream, which sparkled with all colors of the rainbow. But I could not say from which cup it flowed out, nor into which it was flowing.

A direct path went up to great heights on the verge of the horizon, and above there was a great light. And with terror I understood that I had come to the last mysteries, from which there is no return. Hereof is some part of the Secret of Eternal Life, as it is possible to man in his incarnation. All the conventional emblems are renounced herein.

So also are the conventional meanings, which refer to changes in the seasons, perpetual movement of life and even the combination of ideas. It is called Temperance fantastically, because, when the rule of it obtains in our consciousness, it tempers, combines, and harmonizes the psychic and physical natures. Under this rule we know in our rational part something of whence we came and wither we are going.

As I looked at the Angle, at his sings, at his cups, at the rainbow stream between the cups, my human heart fluttered with fear, and my human mind was wrought with the anguish of incomprehension.

"The name of the Angel is Time," said the Voice. "On his forehead is the Circle. This is the sign of Eternity and the sign of Life. In the Angel's hands are two cups. One cup is the past, and the other is the future. The rainbow stream between them is the present. You see that it is flowing in both directions.

"This is Time in its most incomprehensible aspect for man. Men think that everything is incessantly flowing in one direction. They do not see that everything eternally meets, that one thing come from the past and another from the future, and that Time is the multitude of Circles turning in different directions.

"Understand this mystery and learn to distinguish the opposite currents of the rainbow stream of the present."

Interpretation of this fable tells us that Time is not what we think it is. Time is another illusion of the five senses. Time does not exist. There exists no perpetual and eternal appearance and disappearance of phenomena, no ceaselessly flowing fountain of ever appearing and ever vanishing events.

Everything exists always. There exists only one eternal present, the Eternal Now, which the weak and limited mind of the masses can neither grasp nor conceive.

Time is not a condition of the existence of the universe, but only a condition of the perception of the world by our psychic apparatus, which imposes on the world the conditions of Time, since otherwise the psychic apparatus would be unable to conceive it. Man has become so earthly and outward, says Giehtel, that he seeks afar, beyond the starry sky, in the higher eternity, for that which is really quite near him, within the inner center of his own being, within the atom in his body.

The concept of eternity in relation to Time is the same as the concept of a surface in relation to a line. A surface is a quantity incommensurable with a line. Infinity for a line need not necessarily be a line without an end; it may be a surface, that is an infinite number of finite lines. Eternity can be an infinite number of finite "times."

Separate Time is always a complete circle. We can think of Time as a straight line only on the great straight line of the great Time. If the great Time does not exist, every separate Time can be only a circle, that is, a closed curve.

The six-pointed star, which represented the world in ancient symbolism, is in reality the representation of space-time, or the "period of dimensions," i.e., of the three space-dimension and the three time-dimension in their perfect union, where every point of space includes the whole of Time, and every moment of Time includes the whole of space, when everything is everywhere and always. The Laws of Time and Eternity are illogical laws. They cannot be studied with the four rules of arithmetic. In order to understand them, one must be able to think irrationally and without "facts." Nothing is more deceptive than facts, when we cannot have all the facts referring to the matter under discussion and are forced to deal with accessible facts which, instead of helping us, only distort our vision.

And how can we know that we have a sufficient quantity of facts for judgment in one direction or another, if we have no general plan of things and know no general system?

Our so-called scientific system based on facts, are as deficient as the facts themselves. In order to come to the laws of Time and Eternity, we must start with the understanding of that state in which there is no Time and no Eternity opposed to each other.

The Eternal Now is the state of Brahma, the state in which "everything is everywhere and always," that is, in which every point of space touches every point of time, and which is expressed in ancient symbolism by the intersecting triangles, a six-pointed star.

www.ingramcontent.com/pod-product-compliance
Lightning Source LLC
Chambersburg PA
CBHW050556280326
41933CB00011B/1865